OXFORD BOOKWORMS LIBRARY
Factfiles

Brazil

NICK BULLARD

Stage 1 (400 headwords)

T0355248

Series Editor: Rachel Bladon
Founder Factfiles Editor: Christine Lindop

OXFORD
UNIVERSITY PRESS

Great Clarendon Street, Oxford, OX2 6DP, United Kingdom

Oxford University Press is a department of the University of Oxford.
It furthers the University's objective of excellence in research, scholarship,
and education by publishing worldwide. Oxford is a registered trade
mark of Oxford University Press in the UK and in certain other countries

ISBN: 978 0 19 4237949

A complete recording of *Brazil* is available

Printed in China

Word count (main text): 4,951 words

For more information on the Oxford Bookworms Library,
visit www.oup.com/elt/gradedreaders

ACKNOWLEDGEMENTS

*The publisher would like to thank the following for their permission to reproduce
photographs*: Alamy pp.1 (Jan Sochor), 4 (BrazilPhotos.com), 5 (slavery/
Pictorial Press Ltd, Tiradentes/age fotostock Spain, S.L.), 6 (The Art
Archive), 9 (Janine Wiedel Photolibrary), 12 (Jan Sochor), 16 (epa european
pressphoto agency b.v.), 17 (Fabio Pili), 19 (Worldwide Picture Library),
23 (rhea/Peter Llewellyn), 24 (Monica Rua), 25 (jaguar, tapir/Juniors
Bildarchiv GmbH), 27 (piranha/Animal Stock, dolphin/Juniors Bildarchiv
GmbH), 28 (imageBROKER), 31 (dbimages), 32 (Domenico Tondini),
33 (Feijoada/Bon Appetit, Moqueca/Bon Appetit), 42 (Grzegorz Knec),
47 (Amazon/Worldwide Picture Library, stadium/Peter M. Wilson); Corbis
pp.8 (Eliano Rossi), 10 (Yadid Levy), 13 (Alex Robinson), 23 (hummingbird/
Frans Lanting), 30 (Pierre Merimee), 35 (Steve Outram), 47 (carnival/Yadid
Levy); Getty pp.2 (Kean Collection), 7, 11, 21 (Mint Images/Frans Lanting),
27 (anaconda/Pete Oxford), 36 (futsal/AFP), 37 (Antonio Scorza), 38 (Rainer
W. Schlegelmilch), 39, 40 (Nestor J. Beremblum), 41 (Shaun Botterill/FIFA);
Rex Features pp.14 (Sony Pics/Everett), 36 (Pele/Colorsport); Shutterstock
pp.iv, 2, 20, 22, 29, 34, 47 (beach, Ipanema from above).
Illustration by: Lorena Alvarez/The Bright Agency pp.15 (reproduced
from Classic Tales *Rainforest Boy* ISBN 978 0 19 423980 6
© Oxford University Press 2014).

CONTENTS

1	Welcome to Brazil	1
2	Who are the Brazilians?	3
3	Music and celebrations	8
4	Films, books, and art	14
5	Beautiful places	18
6	Animals and plants	23
7	Cities	28
8	Eating and drinking	32
9	Sport	36
10	A world player	40

GLOSSARY	43
ACTIVITIES: Before reading	47
ACTIVITIES: While reading	48
ACTIVITIES: After reading	52
INDEX	57
ABOUT THE BOOKWORMS LIBRARY	60

1   Welcome to Brazil

Brazil has it all. Sun, sea, beautiful beaches – and exciting cities, too. It is the home of Carnival, of samba music and dance, and of the 2014 World Cup and 2016 Olympics. At 8.5 million square kilometres, Brazil is the biggest country in South America and the fifth biggest country in the world.

Most of the north of the country is rainforest, but in the north-east, there is desert: very little rain falls here, and there are only very small trees and plants. Brazil has the biggest wetland in the world; and nearly 7,500 kilometres of coast, with many beautiful islands. So across Brazil, you can see many different kinds of place.

Brazil is a country of different people, too. About 200 million people live there today, and their ancestors came from many places – from other countries in South America, and from Europe, Africa, Asia, and the Middle East. Because of this, Brazil has music, food, and festivals from around the world. There are different languages, too, but everyone speaks Portuguese.

Brazil is a beautiful and interesting country, and it is not like any other place. This, then, is why more than five million people visit every year – and why more and more people want to learn about this amazing country!

2 Who are the Brazilians?

Before Europeans came to Brazil 500 years ago, more than five million people lived there. These people were called the indigenous people – they were born in Brazil, and their ancestors lived there. But everything changed when Pedro Álvares Cabral arrived from Portugal with his men in April 1500.

Brazil became a Portuguese colony – its ruler was now the king of Portugal. Soon, people from Portugal began to come to the new colony, and in 1600, there were about 30,000 Europeans in Brazil. They came because they wanted to find gold and take it back to Europe.

The Portuguese arrive in Brazil

A brazilwood tree

They did not find any gold at first, but they did find brazilwood – a tree with red wood. People in Europe wanted brazilwood because they could dye their clothes – colour them red – with it. So the Portuguese took the trees to Europe and got a lot of money for them. Because of this, they called their new colony 'Brazil'.

Some of Brazil's indigenous people found Portuguese husbands and wives, and had children. But many of the indigenous people died in fights with the Europeans, and many more died because the Portuguese brought new diseases to Brazil.

From the 1550s, the Europeans began to grow sugar on big farms in the north-east of Brazil. Sugar grew well there, so the Europeans needed workers, and they brought slaves from Africa to Brazil in ships. The slaves worked on sugar farms at first, but in about 1695, people found gold in Minas Gerais in south-eastern Brazil, so many slaves went to work there. In the 1800s, people began to need slaves on coffee farms, too. Between 1500 and 1850, more than three million African slaves came to Brazil – so more than half of all Brazilians today have some African ancestors.

Slaves on a coffee farm

In the 1780s, some Brazilians began to want independence from Portugal – they wanted Brazilian rulers for their country, not Portuguese ones. The most important of these people was a man called Tiradentes. He wanted Brazilians to come out into the streets and fight for their independence. When the Portuguese heard about this, they found Tiradentes and then killed him on 21 April 1792. But people did not forget him, and 21 April is an important day in Brazil.

Tiradentes

In 1808, the Portuguese royal family came and lived in Rio de Janeiro. Rio was the capital city of Brazil at that time, and because their royal family was now living in the city, more than 10,000 Portuguese people moved there. Most of the royal family left Rio in 1821, but one prince stayed, and in 1822, he gave Brazil independence.

After 1888, no one in Brazil could have slaves, so Brazil's coffee farmers needed new workers. Between 1820 and 1930, about 4.5 million people moved to Brazil from Europe and found work on farms there. Germans worked on farms in the south of Brazil, and in the late 1800s, many more people came from Portugal, Spain, and Italy.

In 1889, Brazil became a republic – a country without a royal ruler. There were now many Europeans in Brazil, but at about this time, people began to arrive there from other places in the world. From 1908, many Japanese farmers moved to Brazil, because they could not find work at home. Some never went back to Japan, and today there are more than one million Japanese Brazilians. In the 1950s, many Korean people arrived, and in the 1970s and 1980s, a lot of people came from Lebanon, because there was fighting there. So today's Brazilians have ancestors from all around the world.

3   Music and celebrations

Brazilians love to sing and dance, and you can hear music all the time in Brazil – in clubs and restaurants and on the streets and beaches. There are many interesting kinds of Brazilian music, but a lot is dance music, like samba, the music of carnivals.

Samba began in Bahia, in the north-east of Brazil, in the early 1900s, and it grew out of the music of the African slaves. Now, people play samba all around Brazil, and all around the world, too. There are samba clothes, samba schools, and every year, on 2 December, there is a National Samba Day in Brazil.

Samba

Forró music

In the 1950s, the famous musician Luiz Gonzaga took forró music from Pernambuco State in north-eastern Brazil to the cities of Rio de Janeiro and São Paulo. Soon, people all around Brazil began to play it. There are different kinds of forró music, but you always do forró dances in twos. You can move slowly or quickly, near the other dancer or not very near.

Bossa nova became an important kind of music in Brazil in the 1950s and 1960s. It grew out of samba and jazz (music from New Orleans in the 1910s) in places in Rio de Janeiro called Ipanema and Copacabana. When João Gilberto sang the song *Desafinado* in 1958, it became famous around the world, but the most famous bossa nova song today is *The Girl from Ipanema*.

North-eastern Brazil is home to mangue beat. Two musicians, Chico Science and Fred 04, began mangue beat in Recife in the 1990s. It comes from different kinds of modern music and Brazilian music, like samba. Today, there are lots of amazing mangue beat musicians.

Rio Carnival

At Carnival time, there is lots of music and dance in Brazil. Every city has a Carnival, and they are all different. Carnival first came from Europe, and in Brazil African people brought their traditions to it. Today, Carnival is the biggest celebration in the country. Carnival time is in February or March, and in most cities, the celebrations are in the streets.

The biggest and most famous Carnival in the world is in Rio de Janeiro. Artists and samba schools all around the city make the costumes, and they make amazing

moving sculptures called floats, too. There are about 40,000 dancers and musicians in the Rio Carnival, and more than five million people watch it on the streets.

The Carnivals in Salvador and Olinda are very famous, too, and in 2013 more than 2.5 million people went to the Galo da Madrugada in Recife on Carnival Saturday.

There are many more wonderful celebrations in Brazil, too. In Rio de Janeiro on 31 December, millions of people go to Copacabana Beach in the evening. They dance, play music, and wear white clothes. It is one of the best New Year celebrations in the world.

New Year celebrations,
Copacabana Beach

Yemanjá

On 2 February, some towns on the coast of Brazil have special Yemanjá celebrations for the sea. The biggest of these is on the beach in Salvador. People eat, dance, play music, and put flowers and other things into the water.

An important celebration in northern and north-eastern Brazil is Bumba-meu-boi, or Boi Bumbá. At Boi

Boi Bumbá

Bumbá celebrations, people dance and tell stories. The best place for Boi Bumbá celebrations is in the Amazon city of Parintins, because the costumes and the dancing are amazing. But you can find great music and dancing in Brazil in any town and at any time of year!

4 Films, books, and art

Brazilians love going to the cinema, and there are some amazing films by Brazilian film-makers like Walter Salles. Salles's first big film was *Central Station* (1998). In the film, a nine-year-old boy meets a woman called Dora at Central Station, Rio de Janeiro. She helps the boy when his mother dies and he goes looking for his father.

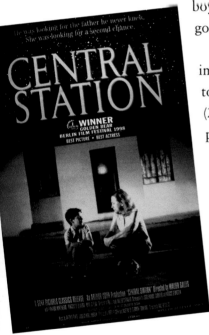

Fernando Meirelles is an important Brazilian film-maker, too. His famous film *City of God* (2002) tells the story of poor people in Rio.

City of God came from a book by the Brazilian writer Paulo Lins – and there are many good Brazilian writers. Three of the most important are Machado de Assis, Jorge Amado, and Paulo Coelho.

Machado de Assis was born in Rio de Janeiro in 1839. His family was poor, so he could not go to good schools, but he learned French, English, German, and later Greek, because he wanted to read the world's best books. He is one of the most famous Brazilian writers.

Jorge Amado (1912–2001) lived on a farm when he was a child, and he wrote his first book when he was only eighteen years old. His most famous book is called *Dona Flor and Her Two Husbands*.

Paulo Coelho (1947–) started writing when he was young, too. Not many people were interested in his story *The Alchemist* when he wrote it in 1988, but later millions of people read the book, and it is now in sixty-seven different languages!

The first Brazilian stories were traditional stories, and many of them are thousands of years old. There are many stories about a boy called Saci Pererê. He has one leg, wears a red hat, and often breaks things. The stories of Saci-Pererê came from the indigenous people of Brazil. There are famous stories about Curupira, too – a boy with red hair and interesting feet – and about the mula-sem-cabeça, a horse without a head.

Curupira

Ernesto Neto
and his sculpture

Brazil is home to some amazing artists. Three of the most famous are Vik Muniz, Beatriz Milhazes, and Ernesto Neto. Vik Muniz makes really interesting pictures from things like sugar, leaves, and coffee, and then takes photos of them. Beatriz Milhazes is from Rio de Janeiro, and her pictures are in beautiful colours, like Carnival costumes. Ernesto Neto is from Rio, too, and he makes wonderful sculptures. You can walk through Ernesto Neto's sculptures and put your hands on them; they take you into a different world.

Every two years, some of the world's most famous and interesting artists visit São Paulo and many people go to see their pictures in an amazing building called the Ciccillo Matarazzo Pavilion. The building is famous in São Paulo, and it was made by Brazil's most important architect: Oscar Niemeyer.

Niemeyer first became famous for some very modern architecture in Pampulha, Belo Horizonte. But most people remember him for his work in Brasília, the new capital city of Brazil. When President Juscelino Kubitschek began to build Brasília in 1956, Niemeyer was the architect for the most important buildings. After this, he made hundreds of buildings in Brazil and all around the world. He finished his last building eight months before he died in 2012 – when he was 104 years old!

Brazil National Congress in Brasília, by Oscar Niemeyer

5 Beautiful places

Brazil has many beautiful places, from islands and beaches to the Amazon Rainforest and the wonderful Iguaçu waterfall.

More than three million square kilometres of the Amazon Rainforest are in Brazil – and about half of Brazil is Amazon Rainforest! It is hot and wet here, so trees and plants grow very quickly, and the tallest trees are forty metres high.

There are not many roads in the rainforest, so people often go from place to place by river. The Amazon River goes across Brazil from east to west, and at 6,400 kilometres long, is one of the two longest rivers in the world. It comes into Brazil at Tabatinga, and you can go from Tabatinga to the mouth of the Amazon at the Atlantic coast in nearly two weeks.

The Amazon Rainforest is home to many plants and animals, and there is important wildlife in Brazil's Atlantic Forest, too. The Atlantic Forest goes for 4,000 kilometres along the coast. It has more than 200 species of birds, and about 8% of all the plant species in the world. Chapada Diamanina National Park in Bahia is also very interesting. There are very big hills there, and many birds and flowers.

Brazil has a long coast, and lots of amazing beaches. Some of Brazil's most famous beaches are in Rio de Janeiro,

The Amazon Rainforest

but there are beautiful beaches from Litoral Gaúcho in the south to Recife and Fortaleza in the north-east. There are some interesting islands along the coast, too. The islands of Fernando de Noronha are about 400 kilometres from Brazil. Only about 2,500 people live on the islands, and there are some amazing animals and plants in the water around them.

There are wonderful islands nearer to the coast, too, like the island of Ilha Grande. It is only 150 kilometres from Rio de Janeiro, but it is very different from the city. There are no cars on Ilha Grande, so it is very quiet. People there can walk through the island's Atlantic Forest, or visit its beautiful beaches.

A Brazilian beach

The Pantanal

Brazil has the biggest wetland in the world – the Pantanal. The Pantanal is about 200,000 square kilometres, and a lot of it is under water for some of the year. Hundreds of different animals live there.

The Iguaçu Falls

There are many wonderful waterfalls on the rivers of Brazil. The highest waterfall in the country is the 353-metre Aracá waterfall, but the Iguaçu Falls, between Argentina and Brazil, are some of the biggest in the world. There are 275 different waterfalls at Iguaçu, and some of them are more than eighty metres high. When you stand next to them, the noise is amazing!

6   Animals and plants

You can see interesting animals and plants all around Brazil. Brazil has more species than nearly any country in the world. Many beautiful birds live here, like hummingbirds, the world's smallest birds – they are only a few centimetres long. Brazil is home to one of the world's biggest birds, too – the rhea. Rheas are more than 1.5 metres tall and they cannot fly. They are endangered – there are not many alive today – because Carnival costumes were often made from their feathers. But now, people want to protect the birds.

A rhea

feathers

A hummingbird

A sloth

Over 30% of all animal species in the world live in the Amazon Rainforest, and different animals live in different places in the forest. Birds and monkeys live up in the tallest trees, and animals like snakes and sloths live in smaller ones. Sloths are like monkeys, but they have very small ears, and they are only about half a metre tall. Sloths move very, very slowly, so small animals and plants can live and grow on them!

A jaguar

A lot of visitors to Brazil want to see jaguars. These beautiful big cats live in the rainforests and wetlands, and the indigenous people tell many stories about them. Jaguars are endangered, so you cannot often see them, but some of the biggest jaguars in the world live in the Pantanal.

The Brazilian tapir is endangered, too. This interesting animal lives in the rainforest, and it is one metre tall. It has a long nose, and it can take fruit and leaves with its nose and put them in its mouth.

A tapir

nose

You can find the world's biggest snake, the green anaconda, in rivers, forests, and wetlands. Anacondas like to wait in the water, and catch animals when they come to drink. They usually eat smaller animals like fish and birds, but some anacondas are nine metres long, and they can eat a tapir or a jaguar!

Everyone knows about piranhas, and these fish live in the rivers of Brazil. They are not very big, but they have a big mouth and a lot of teeth. Piranhas eat fish and other animals, and in some stories and films, they eat people. But in the real world, people more often catch piranhas and eat *them*!

Pink river dolphins live in the Amazon River, and indigenous people tell stories about them. At night, they say, the pink dolphins change into men and visit villages near the river. Then, when the day comes, they change into dolphins again and go back to the water.

In many places around the world, plants and animals are endangered because they are losing their homes – and this is very true in Brazil. Here, forests are becoming smaller: people are cutting down trees because they need wood, or because they want new farms. There are 100,000 square kilometres of Atlantic Forest on the coast of Brazil today, but 500 years ago the forest was ten times bigger. People are cutting down trees in the Amazon Rainforest, too: it is 20% smaller today than it was forty years ago. But more and more, people now want to protect animals and their homes.

A green anaconda

A piranha

A pink dolphin

7   Cities

More than 80% of Brazilians live in cities, and some of these cities are very big. From the beaches of Recife to the parks of Curitiba and the beautiful buildings of Salvador, each Brazilian city is different.

When you fly over the capital city, Brasília, it looks like a picture of a plane – and planes were very important when Brasília was built. President Kubitschek wanted to build the new capital thousands of kilometres from the nearest city, and 500 kilometres from the nearest good road. So the city's builders and architects brought everything in by plane. The new capital city was built by 30,000 workers in only three years. It was built for 500,000 people, but nearly three million live there now.

Brasília

Rio de Janeiro

Before Brasília, Rio de Janeiro was the capital city. Today, it is the most famous city in Brazil, and many people visit it every year. Rio is a city by the sea, and it has beautiful beaches like Copacabana and Ipanema. There are big mountains in Rio, too, and the most famous are Corcovado and Sugarloaf. You can take a train up Corcovado, and look down on the amazing city.

There are interesting museums in Rio, like the National Museum of Brazil. And the city has a national park, too: thirty-two square kilometres of Atlantic Forest, called Tijuca Forest. In Rio, you can swim in Sepetiba Bay, play volleyball on Ipanema Beach, or dance samba in the clubs of Lapa. It is one of the most exciting cities in the world.

There are 6.3 million people in Rio de Janeiro, but 11.3 million people live in São Paulo. It is the biggest city in Brazil, and one of the biggest cities in the world. There are six million cars on the streets of São Paulo, and a thousand more every day. São Paulo began to grow 200 years ago because there were a lot of coffee farms, and today many of Brazil's most important businesses have their offices there.

There are lots of wonderful museums and interesting places in São Paulo, and the Modern Art Museum is the most important in South America. Here you can see work by Brazilian artists like Manabu Mabe, and by European artists from Botticelli to Picasso. Weekends are amazing in São Paulo. You can listen to samba music all around the city on Saturdays, shop and eat in the street, or visit Ibirapuera Park – one of the biggest city parks in South America.

São Paulo

Salvador

Salvador, in the north-east, is Brazil's third biggest city, and one of the oldest cities in the country. It has beautiful old buildings, and it is near to some of the best beaches in Brazil. Many of the slave ships from Africa came to Salvador, and so a lot of the people here have African ancestors. The music and dance feel African, and a lot of the food is African-Brazilian, too.

Manaus is a city in the Amazon Rainforest. Nearly two million Brazilians live in Manaus, and there are no roads from the south of Brazil, so people get there by plane or by river. One hundred years ago, Manaus was one of the richest cities in the world, but then many of its businesses closed, and for a long time, Manaus was poor. Today, it is growing again, and things like CDs, phones, and ships are made there. Thousands of people visit every year, too.

8 Eating and drinking

You can eat good food all around Brazil. At any time of day, when you are hungry, you can always find *pão de queijo* – balls of bread and cheese. Indigenous people made balls of bread thousands of years ago, and when Europeans came to Brazil they began to put cheese into the bread. Today, many Brazilians eat *pão de queijo* for breakfast.

African and European traditions meet in *feijoada*. The Portuguese brought *feijoada* to Brazil, but African people there changed it and it became Brazilian. *Feijoada* is made from meat and beans, and many people eat it every week.

Pão de queijo

beans

Feijoada

A lot of people in Brazil like *moqueca*, too. *Moqueca* is made with fish – so there are always *moqueca* restaurants near the sea. *Moqueca baiana* comes from the north-east of Brazil, but a different kind of moqueca, *moqueca capixaba*, comes from the south-east.

In the south of Brazil, there are a lot of beef farms. The farm workers here are called *gaúchos*, and they go around their farms by horse. *Gaúchos'* traditional food is *churrasco* – a beef barbecue. You can find *churrasco* restaurants all around Brazil, but the best beef comes from the south. *Churrasco* restaurants are often very big, and when people go there they usually eat a lot of meat.

Moqueca

The *gaúchos* also have a hot drink called *mate*. The indigenous people drank *mate* before Europeans came to Brazil, and it is made from the leaves of a South American plant. Usually, people drink it with friends or family, from a *mate* cup. There is only one cup, so one person drinks from it, and then the next person has their *mate* from the cup, too.

But for most Brazilians, the traditional drink is coffee. Today, about 30% of the world's coffee grows in Brazil, and Brazilians drink a lot of it. Most people like to drink a *cafezinho*. A *cafezinho* is a small coffee, without milk, but often with a lot of sugar. Many Brazilians drink four or five *cafezinhos* a day.

A *cafezinho*

juice →

A juice shop

Lots of interesting fruits grow in Brazil, and you can get many good fruit juices there. In most towns, you can find juice shops, and they often have hundreds of different juices. Lots of people like graviola juice, the juice of a big green fruit, and cupuaçu juice from the cupuaçu trees of the rainforest.

Because Brazil has people from many different countries, you can find food from all around the world there. There are many Italian and Japanese restaurants, and hundreds of Lebanese fast food restaurants. You can eat in a 'kilo restaurant', too. Often these places have lots of different kinds of food, and you pay for every kilo. The more you eat, the more you pay!

9   Sport

Pelé

When people think about sport in Brazil, they often remember famous football players like Pelé, Ronaldo, and Kaká. Millions of Brazilians play and watch football, and the Brazilian team is one of the most famous football teams in the world. They won the World Cup for the first time in 1958, and then again in 1962, 1970, 1994, and 2002. Brazilians play *futsal*, too. This is football with a team of only five people.

Children playing *futsal*

Brazil win the
World Cup in 2002

Football first came to Brazil in the 1890s, when British people arrived in São Paulo, but today you can see it all around the country – on TV and in stadiums, on the beach and in the streets. It is amazing when you watch one of the big Brazilian football teams, like São Paulo at the Morumbi Stadium, or Flamengo at the Maracanã Stadium in Rio de Janeiro.

But football is not the only sport in Brazil. Because most Brazilians live on, or near, the coast, many people play beach sports. At the weekends, in places like Rio de Janeiro's Copacabana Beach, there is beach football, beach volleyball, and footvolley. Footvolley is Brazilian, and people played it for the first time on Copacabana Beach about fifty years ago. Footvolley is like volleyball, but you hit the ball with your feet, not your hands.

People play and watch a lot of tennis and basketball in Brazil, too. There are tennis clubs all around the country, and many people remember the famous Brazilian tennis players Maria Esther Bueno and Gustavo Kuerten. Two of the country's best basketball players were Oscar Schmidt and Hortência Marcari. There are lots of very good young players in the sport today, and many Brazilians love basketball.

Brazil is a very good place for motor racing, and every year there is an important motor race called a Grand Prix at Interlagos in São Paulo. Three famous motor racing drivers came from Brazil: Emerson Fittipaldi, Nelson Piquet, and Ayrton Senna. Ayrton Senna was one of the best drivers of all time. He came from São Paulo, and in 1991, he won the Brazilian Grand Prix. When he died in 1994, shops, schools, and businesses closed for three days because people wanted to remember him.

Ayrton Senna

Capoeira

Perhaps the most interesting and traditional Brazilian sport is *capoeira*. *Capoeira* is a martial art – a fighting sport – but when you watch it, it looks like dancing. It is different from most martial arts because there is music. African slaves began *capoeira* hundreds of years ago because they wanted to learn to fight. Today, millions of people around the world learn it. And at weekends in parks all around South America, you can listen to the music and watch this interesting Brazilian sport.

10   A world player

Brazil is becoming more and more important in the world, and it is getting richer. Farming is big business, and Brazilian coffee, sugar, and beef go all around the world. There are many new businesses, too – and Brazil makes planes, computers, and more than three million cars every year.

Brazil is an important world player in sport. The World Cup first came to Brazil in 1950, and many Brazilians were very happy when it came again in 2014. There were thirty-two countries in the 2014 FIFA World Cup, and more than three million tickets for the matches. There was a lot of hard work for

Brazilians when they were getting ready for the World Cup. They had twelve stadiums, from Porto Alegre in the south to Manaus in the north. Some of the stadiums were new, and some, like the famous Maracanã stadium in Rio de Janeiro, were rebuilt for the World Cup. Many more buildings and roads were built in the twelve World Cup cities, too.

In June 2014, about one million people arrived in Brazil from countries all around the world – and about three million Brazilians came to the World Cup cities from their homes across Brazil.

The first match began at 5 p.m. on 12 June 2014 – Brazil played Croatia. Hundreds of millions of people watched when Brazil won that first match, and in the next month, one in every three people in the world watched the World Cup.

In the last match of the World Cup, in Rio de Janeiro, Germany played Argentina, and won. It was an exciting day, after an exciting month of football. Many people wanted Brazil to win the World Cup, and of course that did not happen in 2014. But people around the world saw some very good football in beautiful stadiums. They watched seventy-eight matches, and for many of them, 2014 was the year of the best World Cup.

Germany win the World Cup in Brazil in 2014

In August 2016, the world watches Brazil again when the Olympic Games come to Rio de Janeiro. Brazilians are building new stadiums, and a big Olympic village with thousands of rooms for the sports-people. This is the first Olympic Games in South America, and there are seven million tickets for games in forty-two different sports. So 2016 is going to be an exciting year for Brazil.

With all this, and its beautiful places, interesting traditions, and good music, food, and sport, Brazil is an amazing country – and we are going to hear more and more about it!

GLOSSARY

amazing *(adj)*   exciting and interesting

ancestors *(n)*   people in your family many years ago

architect *(n)*   An architect designs buildings (decides how they must look, how they are made, etc).

architecture *(n)*   the design of a building or buildings

around *(prep)*   on all sides of something

art *(n)*   beautiful things like pictures and sculptures

artist *(n)*   An artist makes art.

barbecue *(n)*   a way of cooking food on a fire

basketball *(n)*   a ball game for two teams; you catch the ball and throw it through a hoop (a big metal ring)

beach *(n)*   a low place next to the sea, with sand or little stones

become *(v)*   to begin to be something (past tense **became**)

beef *(n)*   meat from a cow

business *(n)*   something like a shop or factory; it makes or sells things

capital city *(n)*   the most important city in a country

carnival *(n)*   a party in the streets with music and dancing

celebration *(n)*   doing something special because you are happy or because it is an important time, e.g. a birthday

cheese *(n)*   a yellow or white food; it is made from milk

city *(n)*   a big and important town

coast *(n)*   land next to the sea

costume *(n)*   special clothes for an important time

cut down *(v)*   when you cut something with e.g. a knife and it falls down

dance *(v & n)*   to move your body with music

disease *(n)*   an illness; often it comes to you from another person

farm *(n)*   People keep animals and grow food on a farm.

fight *(n & v)*   when two people push and hit each other (past tense **fought**)

film *(n)*   a story in moving pictures on television or at the cinema

food *(n)*   what people and animals eat

fruit *(n)* sweet food, e.g. oranges and apples; they grow on plants and trees

gold *(n)* an expensive yellow metal; rings etc. are often made of gold

grow *(v)* to become bigger (past tense **grew**)

high *(adj)* far up above the ground

island *(n)* a place with water all around it

kind *(n)* a group of the same things or people

leaf *(n)* A leaf is flat and green and grows on a plant or tree.

match *(n)* a game between two people or teams

modern *(adj)* coming from this time, or from not long ago

motor racing *(n)* In this sport, people drive cars very fast because they want to win races.

mountain *(n)* a very high hill

museum *(n)* In a museum you can look at old or interesting things.

music *(n)* When you sing or play an instrument, e.g. the guitar, you make music.

park *(n)* a place with no buildings in a town or city; people walk and play games there

place *(n)* where something or somebody is

plant *(n)* A plant grows from the ground.

president *(n)* the ruler of a country when there is no king or queen

prince *(n)* usually the son of a king or queen

protect *(v)* to stop people hurting someone or breaking something

rainforest *(n)* a kind of forest in hot places with lots of rain

restaurant *(n)* In a restaurant, you can buy food and eat it.

royal *(adj)* of or about a king or queen and their family

rule *(v)* to control a country (say what its people can or can't do)

sculpture *(n)* a thing made from stone, wood, etc. by an artist

slave *(n)* People buy and sell slaves, and the slaves must work for those people for no money.

species *(n)* a group of the same animals or plants

sport *(n)*   a game or activity like football or running

stadium *(n)*   a place with seats around; you watch sport there

story *(n)*   words by a writer about real or unreal people or things

sugar *(n)*   something sweet from a plant; people put it in food and drinks

team *(n)*   a group of people in a sport or game; they play against another group

tradition *(n)*   When people do something for many years, it becomes a tradition; *(adj)* **traditional**

volleyball *(n)*   a game for two teams; they hit a ball with their hands

waterfall *(n)*   where a river falls from a high place

wetland *(n)*   a place with lots of water

win *(v)*   to be the best or the first in a game, race, or sport (past tense **won**)

wood *(n)*   the hard part of a tree; many tables and chairs are made from wood

world *(n)*   the Earth with all its countries and people

Brazil

ACTIVITIES

ACTIVITIES

Before reading

1 Match the words below to the pictures.

beach   carnival   city   rainforest   stadium   waterfall

1 _____   2 _____   3 _____

4 _____   5 _____   6 _____

2 How much do you know about Brazil? Are these sentences
true or false?

1 Brazil is the biggest country in South America.
2 The only Carnival in Brazil is in Rio de Janeiro.
3 The Amazon River is one of the longest rivers in the
world.
4 The Amazon Rainforest is getting smaller every year.
5 São Paulo is the capital city of Brazil.
6 Brazil was once a Spanish colony.

ACTIVITIES

While reading

Read Chapter 1. Choose the correct words to complete the sentences.

1 The *2014 / 2016* World Cup was in Brazil.
2 Brazil has the biggest *city / wetland* in the world.
3 The ancestors of Brazilians come from all around *South America / the world*.
4 Brazil has *millions / thousands* of visitors every year.

Read Chapter 2. Put the events in order.

a Brazil became a Portuguese colony.
b Brazil became a republic.
c People began to take brazilwood back to Europe.
d Japanese people began to move to Brazil.
e People began to grow sugar in the north-east of Brazil.
f The first Portuguese people came to Brazil.

Now complete these sentences with the years below.

1500   1695   1792   1808   1822

1 In _____, people found gold in Minas Gerais.
2 In _____, the Portuguese royal family came to live in Rio de Janeiro.
3 In _____, Cabral and the Portuguese arrived in Brazil.
4 In _____, Brazil became an independent country.
5 In _____, the Portuguese killed Tiradentes.

Read Chapter 3. Match the words below to the descriptions.

Boi Bumbá   bossa nova   Carnival
forró   samba   Yemanjá

1 a celebration with stories (famous in Parintins)
2 1950s and 1960s music from Ipanema and Copacabana
3 dance music from Bahia, with special clothes etc.
4 the biggest celebration in Brazil
5 the music of Luiz Gonzaga
6 important celebrations for the sea, in February

Read Chapter 4. Complete the sentences with the correct names.

1 _____ is a boy in stories with one leg.
2 _____ did a lot of the architecture in Brasília.
3 _____ made the film *City of God*.
4 _____ makes pictures from leaves, coffee, etc.

Read Chapter 5. Match the two parts of the sentences.

1 The Atlantic Forest…
2 The Amazon River…
3 The Amazon Rainforest…
4 The Pantanal…
5 The Iguaçu Falls…

a is more than 6,000 kilometres long.
b are between Argentina and Brazil.
c has more than 200 species of birds.
d goes across about half of Brazil.
e is the biggest wetland in the world.

Read Chapter 6. Complete the sentences with the names of animals.

1 The world's smallest birds are _____.

2 Some of the biggest _____ in the world live in the Pantanal.

3 _____ move slowly, so plants and animals can grow on them.

4 Some _____ are nine metres long.

5 _____ live in rivers and eat fish and other animals.

6 In some Brazilian stories, the pink _____ changes into a man at night.

Read Chapter 7. Choose the correct answers.

1 How many people live in Brasília?
   a) 500,000
   b) three million

2 What are Corcovado and Sugarloaf?
   a) beaches
   b) mountains

3 What is the biggest city in Brazil?
   a) Rio de Janeiro
   b) São Paulo

4 In Salvador, where are many people's ancestors from?
   a) Africa
   b) Japan

5 Which city has no roads to it from the south of Brazil?
   a) Manaus
   b) Salvador

Read Chapter 8. Complete the sentences with the words below.

cafezinho   churrasco   cupuaçu
feijoada   moqueca   pão de queijo

1 You can make _____ from bread and cheese.
2 There are meat and beans in _____.
3 You can often eat _____ near the sea.
4 The traditional food of *gaúchos* is the _____.
5 A small sweet coffee with no milk is called a
   _____.
6 The _____ is a fruit from the rainforest.

Read Chapter 9. Correct the <u>underlined</u> word in each sentence to make the sentences true.

1 In <u>football</u>, there are five people in a team.
2 People first played footvolley on <u>Maracanã</u> Beach.
3 Oscar Schmidt was a famous <u>tennis</u> player.
4 You can see <u>motor racing</u> in parks all around South America.

Read Chapter 10. Are the sentences true or false?

1 People in countries around the world buy Brazilian coffee, sugar, and beef.
2 Brazil makes cars, buses, planes, and computers.
3 The 1950 World Cup was in Brazil.
4 All the 2014 World Cup matches were in Manaus.
5 The Olympic Games come to Rio de Janeiro in 2018.

ACTIVITIES

After reading

Vocabulary

1 Complete the sentences with the verbs below.

cut down   dance   fight   protect   rule   win

1 Countries must _____ endangered animals.
2 Tiradentes wanted Brazilian people to _____ Brazil.
3 When people _____ trees, many animals lose their homes.
4 Argentina did not _____ the 2014 World Cup.
5 At Carnival time, people like to _____ in the streets.
6 In the 1780s, some Brazilians wanted to _____ for their independence.

2 Are these words sports, places, or animals?

1 island
2 motor racing
3 dolphin
4 volleyball
5 *capoeira*

6 snake
7 beach
8 tennis
9 jaguar
10 stadium

Grammar

1 Complete the sentences with the correct form of the adjectives.

1 The Atlantic Forest is *small / smaller / smallest* than the Amazon Rainforest.

2 The Aracá waterfall is the *high / higher / highest* in Brazil.

3 The *long / longer / longest* river in Brazil is the Amazon.

4 São Paulo is *big / bigger / biggest* than Brasília.

5 Little villages are usually *quiet / quieter / quietest* than cities.

6 Carnivals are sometimes very *noisy / noisier / noisiest*.

2 Complete the sentences with the words below.

after   because   before   so

1 Indigenous people lived in Brazil _____ the Portuguese arrived.

2 _____ 1908, many Japanese people came to Brazil.

3 In the Amazon Rainforest, people often go from place to place by river _____ there are not many roads.

4 Brazilians came from many different countries, _____ in Brazil you can eat food from around the world.

5 _____ 1822, Brazil was not an independent country.

Reading

1 Read the descriptions and write the names of the places.

1 People found gold in this place.

2 Many slaves came to Brazil from here.

3 This was the capital city before Brasília.

4 This is the best place for Boi Bumbá celebrations.

5 This is an island with no cars.

6 This is a city in the Amazon Rainforest.

2 Match the words below to the descriptions.

bossa nova   feijoada   Yemanjá
Curupira   brazilwood   capoeira

1 This is a famous Brazilian sport, with music. It looks like dancing, but it is a martial art.

2 This is a Brazilian tree. The Portuguese made a red dye from it, and it gave Brazil its name.

3 This is a kind of music. It came from samba and jazz, and Joao Gilberto played it.

4 This is a famous celebration for the sea in Brazil. People put flowers and other things into the water.

5 This is a boy from traditional Brazilian stories. He has red hair and interesting feet.

6 Many Brazilian people eat this every week. It is made from meat and beans.

Writing

1 **Read the email below. Where is Josie?**

Hi Alice

I'm on holiday in Brazil. I'm having an amazing time! I'm in a very big, modern city. Near my hotel I can see a big park; it's called Ibirapuera. I can see lots of big buildings, too. There are wonderful museums here, and some good Japanese restaurants. Yesterday, I went to the Modern Art Museum.

Josie

2 **Use these notes and write an email to a friend about the city of Porto Alegre.**

- having wonderful time
- a big city in the south of Brazil
- can see the Guaiba Lake
- good *churrasco* restaurants
- yesterday – Piratini Palace

3 **Write another email to a friend. Write about a different city in Brazil.**

Speaking

1 Underline the words that compare and contrast things.

1 Jorge Amado began writing when he was young, and Paulo Coelho was a young writer, too.

2 The Aracá waterfall is very high, but the Iguaçu Falls are amazing.

3 Footvolley is like volleyball.

4 Rio de Janeiro is more beautiful than São Paulo.

2 Complete these sentences with the underlined words from exercise 1.

1 Rio de Janeiro is _____ my home city.

2 Brazilian food is _____ the food in my country.

3 Football is a good sport, _____ I like basketball more.

4 I'd like to go to Brazil, and I'd like to go to Japan, _____.

3 Discuss the sentences in exercise 2. Which do you agree with? Which do you not agree with?

4 Discuss the questions below with a partner. Use the sentences in exercises 1 and 2 to help you.

1 Which would you like to go to, the Olympics or the World Cup? Why?

2 For a holiday, would you like to go to the mountains or the beach? Why?

3 What kind of food do you like to eat?

4 What kind of music do you like?

INDEX

A

African Brazilians 2, 4, 8, 10, 31–32, 39
Alchemist, The 15
Amado, Jorge 14–15
Amazon Rainforest 2, 18–19, 24, 26, 31
Amazon River 2, 18–19
anacondas 26–27
animals 23–27
Aracá waterfall 22
architecture 17, 28
Argentina 2, 22, 41
artists 16–17, 30
Asian Brazilians 2, 6–7
Assis, Machado de 14
Atlantic Forest 18, 20, 26, 29

B

Bahia 8
basketball 38
beach sports 37
beaches 11–12, 18, 20, 28–29, 31, 37
beans 32–33
beef 33, 40
Belo Horizonte 2, 17
birds 18, 23–24, 26
Boi Bumbá 12–13
books 14–15
bossa nova 9
Brasília 2, 17, 28–29
Brazil National Congress 17
Brazilian football team 36–37, 40–41

brazilwood 4
Bueno, Maria Esther 38
Bumba-meu-boi 12–13

C

Cabral, Pedro Álvares 3
cafezinho 34
capoeira 39
Carnival 10–11
celebrations 10–13
Central Station 14
churrasco 33
Ciccillo Matarazzo Pavilion 17
cinema 14
cities 28–31
City of God 14
Coelho, Paulo 14–15
coffee 4–6, 16, 30, 34, 40
Copacabana 9, 11, 29, 37
Corcovado 29
costumes 10–11, 13, 23
cupuaçu juice 35
Curitiba 28
Curupira 15

D

dancing 1, 8–13, 29, 31, 39
Desafinado 9
dolphins 26–27
Dona Flor and Her Two Husbands 15
drinks 34–35

E

endangered animals 23, 25–26
European colonists 2–6

F

feijoada 32–33
Fernando de Noronha 20
World Cup 1, 40–41
films 14
Fittipaldi, Emerson 38
Flamengo 37
floats 11
food 32–35
football 1, 36–37, 40–41
footvolley 37
forró music 9
Fortaleza 20
fruit juices 35
futsal 36

G

gaúchos 33–34
Gilberto, João 9
Girl from Ipanema, The 9
gold 3–4
Gonzaga, Luiz 9
Grand Prix 38
graviola juice 35
green anacondas 27

H

hummingbirds 23

I

Ibirapuera Park 30
Iguaçu waterfall 18, 22
Ilha Grande 2, 20
independence 5–6
indigenous people 3–5, 15,
   25–26, 32, 34
Interlagos 38
Ipanema 9, 29

islands 1, 20
Italian restaurants 30, 35

J

jaguars 25–26
Japanese Brazilians 6–7

K

Kaká 36
kilo restaurants 35
Korean Brazilians 7
Kubitschek, Juscelino 17, 28
Kuerten, Gustavo 38

L

Lapa 29
Lebanese Brazilians 7
Mabe, Manabu 30
Manaus 2, 31, 40
mangue beat 9
map of Brazil 2
Maracanã Stadium 37, 41
Marcari, Hortência 38
mate 34
Meirelles, Fernando 14
Middle Eastern Brazilians 2, 7
Milhazes, Beatriz 16
Minas Gerais 4
Modern Art Museum 30
monkeys 24
moqueca 33
Morumbi Stadium 37
motor racing 38
mountains 29
mula-sem-cabeça 15
Muniz, Vik 16
museums 29, 30
music 1–2, 8–13, 30–31, 39

N

National Museum of Brazil 29
National Samba Day 8
Neto, Ernesto 16
New Year celebrations 11
Niemeyer, Oscar 17

O

Olympic Games (2016) 1, 42

P

Pampulha, Belo Horizonte 17
Pantanal 2, 21,25
pão de queijo 32
Parintins 13
parks 28, 30, 39
Pelé 36
Pernambuco State 9
pink dolphins 26–27
Piquet, Nelson 38
piranhas 26, 27
plants 1, 18, 20, 24, 26
Porto Alegre 40
Portuguese royal family 6
Portuguese colonists 4–6
president 17, 28

R

rainforest 1, 18–19, 24–26, 31
Recife 2, 9, 20, 28
republic 6
restaurants 33, 35
rheas 23
Rio Carnival 10–11
Rio de Janeiro 2, 6, 9, 10–11,
    14, 16, 20, 29–30, 37, 41–42
rivers 2, 18, 22, 26
Ronaldo 36

S

Saci-Pererê 15
Salles, Walter 14
Salvador 2, 12, 20, 31
samba 8–11, 28, 30
São Paulo 2, 9, 17, 30, 37–38
Schmidt, Oscar 38
sculptures 16
Senna, Ayrton 38
Sepetiba Bay 29
slaves 4–6, 8, 31, 39
sloths 24
snakes 24, 26–27
sport 36–39, 40–41
stories 13, 15, 25–26
sugar 4, 16, 34, 40
Sugarloaf 29

T

Tabatinga 18
tapirs 25–26
tennis 38
Tijuca Forest 29
Tiradentes 5
trees 1, 4, 18–19, 24, 26

V

volleyball 29, 37

W

waterfalls 22
wetland 1, 21, 25–26
World Cup (2014) 1, 40–41

Y

Yemanjá 12

THE OXFORD BOOKWORMS LIBRARY

THE OXFORD BOOKWORMS LIBRARY is a best-selling series of graded readers which provides authentic and enjoyable reading in English. It includes a wide range of original and adapted texts: classic and modern fiction, non-fiction, and plays. There are more than 250 Bookworms to choose from, in seven carefully graded language stages that go from beginner to advanced level.

Each Bookworms Factfile has full colour photographs, and offers extensive support, including:

▸ extra support pages, including a glossary of above-level words
▸ activities to develop language and communication skills
▸ a complete audio recording
▸ online tests

Each Bookworm pack contains a reader and audio.

4	**STAGE 4**	▸ 1400 HEADWORDS ▸ CEFR B1–B2
3	**STAGE 3**	▸ 1000 HEADWORDS ▸ CEFR B1
2	**STAGE 2**	▸ 700 HEADWORDS ▸ CEFR A2–B1
1	**STAGE 1**	▸ 400 HEADWORDS ▸ CEFR A1–A2

Find a full list of *Bookworms* and resources at
www.oup.com/elt/gradedreaders

If you liked this stage 1 Factfile,
why not try...

Japan
RACHEL BLADON

From sumo wrestlers to robots, Japan has something amazing for everybody.